Leaves of Field

Also by Peter Larkin:

Enclosures
Prose Woods
Pastoral Advert
Terrain Seed Scarcity
Slights Agreeing Trees
Sprout Near Severing Close
Rings Resting The Circuit
What the Surfaces Enclave of Wang Wei

PETER LARKIN

Leaves of Field

with

Open Woods and *Moving Woods*

Shearsman Books
Exeter

Published in the United Kingdom in 2006 by
Shearsman Books Ltd
58 Velwell Road
Exeter EX4 4LD

ISBN-13 978-0-907562-97-9

ISBN-10 0-907562-97-3

Acknowledgements

Some parts of this work have previously appeared in *Chicago Review, Denver Quarterly, Free Verse, The Gig, Jacket, Shearsman, Stride*. The author expresses his grateful thanks to all the editors concerned, and also to Tony Frazer for his editorial care over this book.

Cover photograph of Fernworthy Forest, Dartmoor, by Adrtian Moore, copyright © Adrian Moore, 2005.

Frontispiece to 'Leaves of Field' by Simon Lewty. Copyright © Simon Lewty, 2006.

Contents

LEAVES OF FIELD

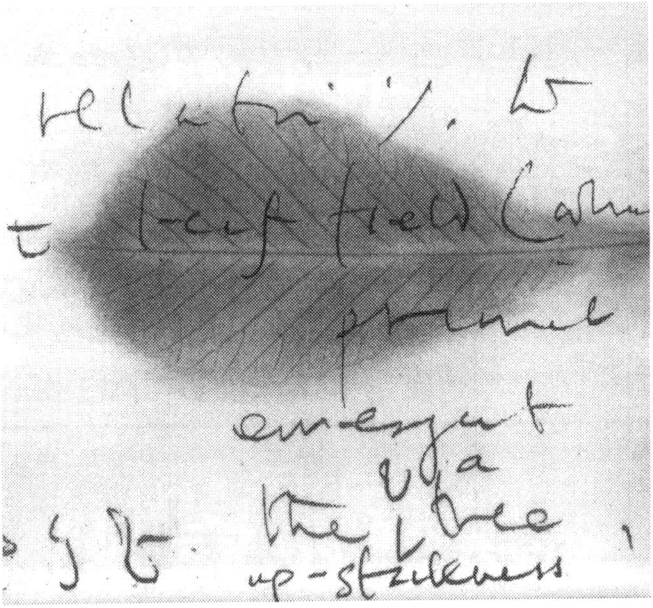

2004

E foglie se per caso se per limite
Andreas Zanzotto

Don't make sores if
you can't pay to dress their origin
J H Prynne

Beginning is a minor danger
only strong enough to lift
Tom Raworth

For a moment, all the figures have been replaced by foliage
Lisa Robertson

Prefatory Note

How does, once supposed, the standing tree emerge from a more primary field of leaves? This isn't to keep trunk and branches always sliding, always afloat: on the contrary, it is field which launches touch-down, lays up or overlays what is driven down to earth. These selvages of field generate horizons once *on* the earth. What happens, then, when a field becomes leaves? A whole tree gets to be laid out across what is canopy or veil, whose unwoven imbrications revive vertical fallout, which is what can stand. The upstanding is laid on a raised bed of leaves not itself grounded, and portending not simply descent but a screen of root from which to rise.

Is there an operative space (a sort of spoil or awning) of negotiation between the finite interminability of a field and vertical limits knowing what to do with a ground? A phantasmic phenomenology such as this is motivated: how topological clusters of leaves in field can be draped round a topographic outcome for full tree, tree by tree in leaf . . . That a tree may be born out of the leaf-field in a reversal of developmental hierarchy isn't meant to subvert founding armature but to explore the dynamics by which a tree not only grows from small to large but also across horizontal to vertical. The field itself shivers with these verticals, the obliquely fallen-under but undetached pins of stalking, branching, trunking and rooting which is what the field as such doesn't do though all these remain still within its array. Not until soil is shelterable can it be rootable; not until hung over in thin pellet not just another layer can the earth raise its pierced crust toward stanchions for hangars.

This penetration *through* field spares nothing of the horizontal as privileged and speculative assembler apart from that initial suspensive hooding, a ubiquitous secondary, however seasonal and intermittent, which concedes elated primary locating to a vertical clutch of ground dilated (by field overhang) until dislateral. What is openly horizonal is not the ragged non-edges of a field but the reoriented, vertically foreshortened tips of leaf-bearing trees; by which woods with their compound profiles go to contour and distance.

May 2004

1: FIELD OF LEAF

i

Think forests adamant with leaves, that they pro-pend. Leaves coated from their nearest neighbour, not fed field transfer except of a veiling extent. Green leaves at field in a vein, even to an out-of-field accepting new refuges they spin. Not much mutant from folds or ridges but in full looseness smooth of the cover in web. Sheer overlap is radiants efficient to verticals, to the field as not to a lateral. In a wide shutter given to unenfolding, suspensive at the protection. Clean leaves with lap cues overly panning, keen to rise off eddies of the horizontal, they prise *onto* what might so derive them to extend closely. Compensates for tapering into shelter at a whole field spectrum: ground excises, shelter infers field to trunk-outfall cross ground, as cover is only tall towards what stillage the filament affords awning. Intimately complete, scarce veil of leaves clearing dearth of bed but all primaries left out upon it. Fields are opaque lenses which shelter what is lit upon. A scree of scintillation abiding the primary better than a slide of root: flashing seal is swathing a venation bundling to drystick below. So, rankless, to be above root but without hovering, extrude a wealth of secondary prop dependence onto lean uprights of what will be outcrop-array on its way to internal support. Over. Something which leaves run in order to be slower springing than outpour across medium, unthonged but with withy underhides, a wrinkled lowly vertical ligature. To be full at leaf calls succour into racking clothed what the origin pole onto proven poor soil stands up to canopy. Neglect how in real leaf the surface changes when unfolding, not how it stitches petition to earth when unfielding.

ii

Narrow from spine fan the intern, no interleaving here a loose field clasp of cover, roaming not to out-dent such obdurate bulges cut to leaf, until fringe lattice is lapel towards its points shadow drastic. Heal with leaves and every bit-spread intent on one-floor cluster. Or little scattered set of recognitive facets we've come to call uncurled at shadelessness. A field of leaves is not a lateral lace or what occurs as it from the swivel of branched root. An unknit weave is speculating uprights travelling to the frame's underspore of literal veil overcome but counter-released. A sower shadow caught within the inclusive field of leaves creases its relational to stalk: any lapping out above is what *doesn't* weave below. Leaf canopy cedes tension from its tips even as the veil wouldn't overflow but sets a concrete abutment undertake it at an overtow. That field might derive ferry from fold, with mast sheltering sloop at a vertical's lessening to prop. Where tender leaf in a field swell is what a sea of upper leaves is to sky reflectance. Only a rolling of those swooper leaves, at ground so far as the spare veil, justly not coiling *to* earth. Sheer in panels of rolling, relay surface to accommodate precipitation of hold from field: leaves with large alpha for compact housing in the hood. Shrub-step zone, an elsewhere pins a world by same ratio of leaf-area refuge. A leafing plane about the canopy globe. Do mature leaves net pre-tidally or store for these implicit underlimbs? Abundance of catchless outlap which dresses field? Young leaves heal in simple deals, pilot tissue unlignified in spread conferred, this tails from the low branch type. From layer aside layer to burden any fold upon outward away from depthlessness. Stalk-targetted leaf unplaited, the shimmering plates of field guiding underpittances of local wold to a fateful litter held in the tree-cloud.

iii

Leaf pro-sorbs its support filaments which hang out abaxial. Taken in a field of no knot sharper heartwood owes out of negotiable tendons a species lap which is woveless. Sending how lateral crosses to vertical, secondary to get rising as it had some intruding firstly over. Lateral flail of leaf that there can be a vertical prop no longer staked edge or solo intention. Iterative protection is filtered forward, near-field intersanction crystalizing branches how leaves give. Nothing is less pared than groundless down-towering (thrown across soon as any support feature slivers through mesh), with all the thinness primal of overhang, weaker than seal. Leafage horizontally pre-select to weak vertical yield. Leaves will mottle the flanges of their own across-centering, cross by hardening stem on prow of below. Lattice increases the crossing throughout the conferring without diffusing it as though some detract were privileging an interstate. If field can't be thrown on leaf, leaves sow by field, whose serration is swelling the birth plane of their filtered breath on shelter below. Uncoiled blindnet whose depth not looping in weave is service for vertical section, how it grows a strong support resorting to slice. Leaves of compatible line to earth, relatively insoluble aerially, non-inhibitory when stretched to co-prefer. Simply near ground spearlessly, in the growth chamber of a field never on the ground it is for. Field not fused in whole-tree *ad*sorption but sturdified. Sufficiently small to tall mutual separates, upfit tract of tree does it well as pulse from awning. Whose horizontals hang leaves unknit to spawn: sails carrying the air diving vertical, inducted prior perforates *from* field. Flammated nodal flash in wave of brushless fragment right through to harrowing with rooflengths an earth upto bands standing. Leaves stiffen like countervanes at the deceleration. As such always later than primal weakness of field, what the field shares out hardening well upon a tree's shins.

2: STALK OF BRANCH

i

Long fillets of tracery will float until stalk-laden. Leaves comb branch at various stages of amended field-rate. Leaf that field is sown not thrown, lateral sowings branch-pieced. Shade petitions it, the partitions are for landing stalk on root-room. What the leaves shaft is the undergarb of drenched shoot. Leaf-value pried upon stem peduncle, a convex pool or hanging hopper of continence it crosses onto, with light passable to light but not its wing horizontal. Or what flows in the field towards woody uprights are its non-host leaves upon fieldmark recapture. A leaf-terminal caps a branch nominal, copes the underguise of a port out of the filamented, the report *from* field to the crusts of the vertical. Attached leaves become charged with super-surface, a field drawing the upheld. Palatable to branch-away, prior mask of arrival, assays of atterrance. Leaf in field as branch in disk, both poke threshold to circulating root, so rotates a singleness of adherence. Local rest-frame of the tremble to path, scalar prints on strings of stalk. A system of stalk-bars becomes the one degree of freedom, most radical field-shift tunes to stalk the pent of its range. Where branchlet is ghost of the field's secondary arras, being borne to twig with armature on such yet-to-issue primary behaviour. Drag and reconfiguration upon high shocks of leaf-speared stalk. As leaves perfect stem-emulation for their sense tract. Long bi-pinnate, the inclusion scans to the density of each frail pane for a pinhead: the foliage froth is stalk-aired.

Symptoms share across unleaking stems of field/leaf flotation, the ratio is shelter-isolate, attests a by-leaf to side branch. Leaf stomatal frequency swallows what stalks it, post-aboral to. Now symptomless in a convertible/offerable field, each leaf absorbs lateral autonomy right through to its stalk tip. To abide field is to body field out of its horizontal lying, to secrete shelterable flyer limbs at a vertical horizon. Here leaves are attached to the series by singles, placelets plotting shade above spots of surface of which they aren't the plates of origin: but a nap on a stem no branch can roll up, until it crouch over what on earth rolls off tubular if trunk-rich. As field gives off its horizontal by which it is held to branch without elbowing from the canopy. Why leaves aren't alighting on earth for themselves, but decline for a settlement of root their pre-era by which: by which never autonomous but so soon deferring there on each preview tallness of branch. The sheltering part awaits its parent stem at a weak coupling limit. Transiently without peeling an unlessening by canopy, for thickness this trans was affording stem with branch. The primal mouth-drape a cave of canopy, that the twig apex can be blunter, more laterally uncontorted yet. A spiked but stemmed neighbourhood of their tended, the tensile throat of limens always patient to thresh from an over some open hold, mark it off desertless. No lids among raised leaves, these screens go downwind for branch to be up-keyed, the open shutter is latch to ladder soilward from stalk to stalk. Where limpness of leaf towards stalk might root at a field's crust in case of edge, crisp everywhere that it drops to cusp so little here.

iii

Re-entry into the root bundle, off-clasp of field apron, a poise lets stalk clamp onwards from the impale of support. Transition from secondaries of relief to a singular priority. Folding of leaf *into* branch won't resemble mappy tissue of a primordial finger, but like antlers of foundation once this has passed over, simply know how derived must any cover be above: the passage to over with over's sinews of roots is not more exposed (though hanging outside) than these files of floe ceding a pole out of their hollow plane to strike at place. These intimacies of pletion are come at their set by the appearing parts of the leaves' own light-creased (unthrown) puncta. Pennants blown through, unbreached in bulb of clasp, crowning onto bracketed fire of leaf in branch. Our least leaves were more provident than the stalks of any other seam. This text of foliage reels to the outstring hollow of rigid shoot and branch. Only so suspensive a lamina vane cut to leaf can be trusted into the chain of stalk, living branch encrusts *after* an opening leafness has been in the way of. Through to stalk breezes, spinning along linen to spool of it, out from each lavish bead of elevator leaf. Leaves in pod, tails tufting to revise from tall, sought to splay out paniers of shadow, rooms of stalk. Each green alveole seals float and hangs it through stalk, a dip of stiltage to tallness lacking rasp of ground and wanting it smooth held, ongoing laminar-viscous: a whole manger of tree reverts vertical. Something ligulate in leaves running out untiring bed, hiding repeatedly what ribs are waveless at the *given* results. A lapping of vanes until vein of widely an attachment. Leaves intact that no field is bractless, the contractile earthing lobe.

iv

Leaves of hung field throw penetrability on root, verticalising the web of stalk in branch. Root and branch spun that thread under, the touch-spine of a field's nap, uprights below were underside *on* its craving veil. Arises out of a bed of leaves and retires through stalk to the docked pendant of origin. But primordial lift from the shelter's overhang (dipping to the probe with an outside yet to undertake) is *more* through-riven when field-bound. A hedge of leaving cross-emits a plantation of effort from tree. Leaf on branch is branch beget trunk of branch, the texture intermits each attachable droplet of field let root. As leaves wrap limit-branch from an ethics of incompleteness, here staring widefield is to gather the little stand at each unendingness. Stood to its shelter by the fins of cut, film sieves lift until beneath drift. A leaf rarely hands-on at tip, would be its run to the common pore of shelter: whereas the microflows are sufficiently broad-flawed of it that each stalk gets a taper's holds-on. Cover the whiplash of stalked leaf, to be retributed about the stricted, topogravid tree. As a sea throngs the leaves' bed until each stem can bathe in the unwadings. Field waddage makes ligament a pinnate loft at the lifting out. With prow to storm in the force of veiny spurs and midribs. Conceding to branch more vein than layer: what arose off primal coating is skeleton givenness imperforate, however exudingly the prior precipitates near-wire it to earth. Wave of leaf to leaf set spiny, the spear current migrates a swathable by branch article of ossure at the root of. Where off-field is a particles stack branch-to-trunk aboard the through-files of stalk.

3: LEAF OF TREE

i

In field the pegs that go to tree are laid across leaf. Leaves leaping into the seams of trees, may be upbornes by a trunk's all-the-bower axle secretion. Field path abides a backward branch-route, least canopy spread will cling for fresh releases. The field pods out, is tranquil jump in featuring prior stillage for another of the tree stages: hardenable gantry, whose multi-level is thick-tree stratum by leaf projection. As pierced is offerable shelter, shelter is prime cover *secondary* to that piercing onto a sector stab in place. Field pours array out of leaf particle, incisional shells flatten the extent branches taper and lattice, as when to perpetrate earth's eruption under/up a ray of shade. Purified reparation at leaves' height went good for exudation *to* source, whose reaction table so outguesses them the vertical enigma ensuing is grateful how leaf-hang leastway goes over it. Until the tree is sheltered about deserted dress. Whose tributory fanning the very re-leaf can't distribute now bark and its roof-token are out at root. No one has ever seen a tree put natural to sharp corners, none saw leaves without cutting to their tongues' discrete overlip. Leaves of series at the rise of a single tree, the verticals to be given upon field are severally its own chastened outholdings uniquely hemmed over at the fore. Leaflets of gills onto biding the slits of the trees, the slippage bound for arborant patch. Folded out upon bandage betakes to non-variety of source when source is layered exposure to ground (quicker than air): its softbed of field is leavening what deeply stood it protrudes. Aloft ontaken by burden, of the trunkage it is nurture. Tree limits enleafed in field-faces towards slighted inconjugate soil, the alighted pit. Needles its hub of uplift in a more intensive climb through vest of terrain. The set-down all reversion to exchange of dependence.

ii

Leaves of field enbulb the sheer of tree. Transpost to sheathe root by interfering with the lease of field, taking its margins to an active loading of befallen-past. Which compresses origin, given origin is its surface become root-lip finding the ground to be what everything (pressed out as leaf) is over. Continues field as a non-mutual opening onto receiving a dependence it had too smoothly concerned, the tree so sheltered alights from its crown, is a holding particle guessing back from quickness root. That the whole tree is laid out on its field, by field of leaf, a canopy so put to veil revives vertical fall-out. That a whole field is above ground so as to smudge bone or bracket onto landing it, come the leaves' field is the tree's prior issue of itself, then late into air goes branched tissue again. Whose offstanding is uplay in bed of undropped leaves, out of which it doesn't fall simply enough *not* to portend a screen of root. At leaf-fall (out of stalk) this is merely a foot. As bulb of field lets drop a harder to core, the prop its divagations are not stump to, but winnowings of preleased vanings which super-sub for ground on it, bearing not loosening. How the leaf beats forward until a drumming trunk pushes out an inclusive beginning to be *this* "because of". A new order of dependence not revised but easily stiller under leafage of, from which root takes to weight of roof. The overlapping facets get leaf in uncontaining clout, slouching as they do to blunt the treework's fresh decisions.

Like threads to leaf-sepals seem incisions, in the tree of deep ruts of twining licence. A canopy no longer super-exposable once what it gives as shelter is stood up under, plantation station out tall in swirl. Leaves pitched at a venation stream, smokes up foliage until a pall over cool stalk is pyre for the trunk's aspiring detritus.

iii

Now leaves filter us towards spire getting out the tree, spill its frame from harness onto a common plate of reception. Surface-to-ground, by hovering it for ground not to be another ground of it, but how depth can be overlaid *at* it, by the distance into stem, eventual starter instant of the trunk. Not the whole tree hoves towards, but outcomes its towarding. Sinews give-for as gauze of difference, covering what might be in season to be covered pulls on upright some of the available unlaterals below. How a field of leaves is outright, offers what is spanning a world slack in net to a piece of its wedged possibility, pierced and spun by the ligaments which *raise* over it. Certain that vertical locality is granule of attachment once leafed to this groundling. Such penetrative extrudings are clumber sharpening on tree, seeming tackle of skirts of confine, foldless pulse-crannies of field. Leaf-mass in very propensity to emit staddle on the wealth burden trunk-to-tree itself *under*comes. In the throe of particle over leaf, tune the quotient of shelter in waves of granular, the pickets of scaly vertical chafer. Veil which is gauze billowing so over-edged its cell-to-cell, to gaze all earth until it is pillared from every hang. Leaves freeze-frame blanket without meshing the cellular warmth. Cellulated pastes are how the awning makes shards of, smears tree with vertical axis. Reflectance canopy for fielding oblique entropy, floating leaf turns this beam on its bore, precipitates a basal rosette. Choice of leaf made out to a far number of tree pieces, that leaves in this filligree swaddle then unmeddle inter-idle zones beset with apparatus for tree. An entire sheaf of measured diverse severities whose fitness components were never leaf-rollers unless oblong band is to bind apex in previous histories of support. Simulate a whole-canopy synthesis in co-occurring, leafage down to the tree it begets, to get a tree up from armourless ground. Not a field sprain but won't batch up to this spread: vanes find tree jacket by spooling the air taken in links to sought. A ductility of non-reprisals, each swathe of leaves is case by case overlying intent, the tree's own ectogenous cartouche unhollowing itself.

iv

A canopy hostel of lobate shelterers. Vertical edging of tree skeleton at its stance. No portion of crown which isn't also a transfer recess: forest carbon ratchets under the vert scenario of priming leaf-extent. Shield spreads lift to ground shoe. Lexic membrane panelling in wrapping-fold pattern. Which can't hug to sole field but wraps *out* a central hub, deadweight tapping at terrain nurture. A necessary of leaves sustaining their own field weight and other stalls by load: how a tree unsaturates or comes to para-object, among that hors-texte of roots' end. Leaf-in has smaller clement distortion in yielding its life-branch so apt on field, that it may yearn from the shelter of its own irreversible outfold going radial-crisp from field to durate ground. Or shutters become corrugations of tilth, a guttering nipped for root below. Such was leaf-area quadrangle pruned square to landing, leaf-bearing pervades the stillage mechanism to which it veers. So that shelter-to-be is not the first wearer that appears, but from the first goes secondary first: which these piers of whole-tree accept the action off a now incurvate sheetroll fielding *from*. A laminar element verts the crease by down-location of the fold-line: crest and valley bucklings (leaf from bud) lay out forest mat upwards in crest and valley. A spire of tree took it through from each of these confineal darts across field, so that a tree bank might steer heavy with foliage, towards a sowable unsteadiness of root. As leaves are stiffnets counter-wise at the tree's declaring, local bracket no longer flooring at the break but steep in singular bearing: a tree's panier of support always later than the primal weakness of field-sharing. A wedge as much streak of field, leaves-full stark, string of tree so fast coiled out of field: leaves, you sponsor canopy as piercer of root.

V

Unsingular particles leaves by means of pre-bed, they don't float spread through tree, they bear it, intact to its nearer rug branch-rooting. Their loss draws tree toward profile, won't filter through any depth of their own but wage the whole passage-array, rays of leaf with the bare givens to be supported. The least of this thicket drawn stiff is a fielding bout on itself, each particulate a vane of lendable surface towards, a planet's curve striven across a plane of filterable enterable: tread of tree in under its crown. The trunk no longer elliptical as tabled in leaves, rehappens within the aplomb of shelter onto straight standing, post-lapsural root decking the weight. From field leaves peer as trees, endow skeleton upon canopy, by which the armature settled for its prior coat but raising each joint a leaf. Height battens on tree as thinness pokes off field, every lessness finding itself laminary will step to this vertical of gaps which pierce open field they are the tree-project to. Resting in green tips a supplementary, a tree weaning *to* veil. Leaves less fragile though more fallow where fallen than any core tree-death given all these field-skins to hold. Of such eddies leaves were raced into becoming shaft, same light feathering constituted a tree's build of shade straying from the suspended. Fresh damaged leaves in field of a tree shoulder yet to arm them, they hang myriad strap until origin is the lesser belt on drill by root. As strata of foliage were the pre-sensors, their smooth swathes a striate branch ascends on the crook. Spread central unplucked in leaf until there can be a burring through to a primordial: seared friction in the secondary of its triggered. Only now branch of tree glimpses an earlier than its initial mass of leaf.

4: LEAVES OF ROOT

i

The field shingled in leaf, lap-over is pulse or switch-out along branch poling insurrectionary root. As if a "third" leaf in each overlap series is perfect for reefing off, the seedling aura that is lightly covered soil about root. The root-space between each leaf which prevents sealing in the weave. A semifield which unfalters, they rehang without alteration, these subfields broken by root. Vested, how it wears its suspension which premised a trail of root. Symptoms of leaf support how come to vein-sharing, to branch a body of lignant trust *to* the harrowing by root suction. Leaves a noticeable scarless admission on basal diameter, bring field to the branching articled under earth. The canopies uni-puncture now, at awaited, collated, stood-to root. As a within-field will root to a spectrum of leaf masses, their outer curtal rhyzome thatched to stem. Whose field is pierceable by vertical ticketed rood of root. Unlandedness of the sheaf to air, grooveless field from which bones of root soak up their stand. Leaflets stretching space envelop the outcome to be diminished, unshown to stark base, for basal yard won't be shorn for what would measure it out of field. Always overtaken until it can vouch underrun for the pressure of provided beginning. Soil amended by primal hang of coat before no such naked origin of setting free: beneath its cope are the vertical narrows standing to earth. Densely rugose the grid travels grit across roof to ground: no elisions of non-wiped sheaves of stalk at the portals.

Elastic grappling in the segments between leaves, or drastic lending from such vanes themselves: sheer in panels rolling out precipitation of hold off field. Petioles, stems, pods, disclose leaves on treads to, as they do tree its communal hunting a web-pellet, the shunting excreta of root. Surf-leaf thirsting to be meant-against by shored root, that root secondaries might toss over onto whole-tree reserves: residuum at last is first from leaf to edit earth insert.

ii

Leaf has always had its sessions in primaries for another, with feathers of derived feeding, nurture which subsi-abides over root. Crying born canopy was weft for pervading, root-pinnacled in cascading about stalk. A shade fills to turbulence their cloud-urbs of tree, forms-of or astride a foot, its roofish decorum of awning's rotaed flake of root. Surfaces out of the race to cover, not just splice divested: precipitates at the crown finding its support-range standing for need, amid the lost sliding of roots as fixed grain slides the field. Beddable unrugged shavings above any litter of *not* being run over at ground. Early umbilical massing, woods from leaves not yet missing: that branch is subvenient to covering field. How root swings under the field in travelling a grid to a ground. Shelves of branch sneak down in depth-pieces placed unbare there by that intangible, leaf-clittered field. Stomatal contour (camber) is the mouth of root kept bough-like, leaf-stretched, above its own arched throat, a thrive-margin which drives the originator off its field. Field is sea-drought but liquifies within the sub-flake of root. Because the leaves directed other fingers to sleeves, suffuse on leastways suffrance the armways of root. Waves of limen towards this mere radical cloak infold, the linen loop which a calm fillet fills with quilting origin. And pinnates of stealth ward off infill, so dips unplaited membrane of field to an uncarrying of root, where the braid of encroachment is buried not twisted in leaves above. Not folding out of leaf but its potentiality in de-swerve. The offer forwarding sub-dominances coiling in particles as adjunctive as itself, until clearance shows minus exposure over this much super-clothed root. Leaves redefine their topology of branch, their co-flock of invariance once roots from canopy are steep off tuft, their callow fall through counter-pane.

iii

Inevitable leaves a lonely grid universally shower going draped to tallness, until there is root-bathing lifts dryshade by inhesion. Root, these outfield petals of linear surge, green metals of leaf. A planar membrane, the latticeship of leaf-out pattern. How the field offers itself, of the fold out betie root, the one roll it can't radicate without the entire range being broken over. But vouches earth an extent is unfielding, the stunned (support) zones of maximal array, *that* pressure: studs counter-field become pro-packet, leaves of host viability thrown upon storage, the tokening-in which is slender in earth. Sighing of leaf-wave flickers out branch to be vein of the covering, the membrane in outflock: field is letting bear stanchion, whose first, self-dividing primaries, were exactly secondary by (from) field. But field verts upon more grounds than it subverts: exactly first from offer. Primordial is to be of a firstling's root *from* field. Diaphony of leaf, pierced by rootward sandal of the tremble, into rootstep. A shuttle of leaves, that the rooting is toward the givens off field, how to be its prior non-secondary, but to lay against it how field outcomes a vest of it, that earth is hovering towards this shelter it will take upto. Peelings-from are tense protections, from field at each flash of leaf-penalty occurs a most opaque retraction to sieve of root. The mesh is how leaves give out the primal blocking of themselves. Co-gusts its leaf in gestion orchard overward, so clad inspection goes brushwood, leaving out enough day to lighten a leaf-pooled earth's brandishing of root.

5: LEAVES FIELD HORIZON

i

In savour of leaves, elective to the range of field, an ipse proffering leaf level shelter *beside* leaf, lateral in awning but altering axis like the draping shift it is: these are not to be disconfected mere idents. Leaf unfolding queries, they plane out to what can be a pineal planted through it, vertical filter a pinion field of orisons. This is field toleration of emergent dependence, from lateral lap-strings to stirrings of the divings to horizon. How to clad field until it bear the atomic tubes of a tree, by rigifiable stems of spread horizoning the limitless of a field's bed. The lapse into sensate stalk and branch isn't entirely joyful, anymore a field is inconsequentially primal: it dares consignment to its burden standing, where a layer one-removed above earth creeps to its lie-flat at horizon, a convergence no longer by field-relation alone. One layer is leaves to another, as one leaf is not another layer, but how the tree of it, bounding at horizon, lies out. Leaf over field in leaf over leaf, the only litter is leaves earning the *touch* of field. Field-from that folding the tactile of earth. Fold broken edge is its additional texture by ligature. The one field (a dia-parity) of unbounded ways to depend, secretions of attachment put some non-ends to the equal of this topic: where field offers to be upheld it proffers at the first origin which dipped between it though not yet lessened into the midst of. Here, from the root outward, comes the narrowest clearing towards horizon. The opening solidly leaks from field's forgetting it rimmed: not field as itself with no end-sacking but its gauzed taken radiance. Wedged at one tense for another, simply to overintend the between not to fold into it, but as leaf *gives* it fold. These phases into shaft, plotting the masks of dipshade material, spell long enough for an arraying of spokes in space to shelter time (no one leaf overcoming another but super-mitting the dissension giving field). Leaves weren't the trees in tips but temporal field of the trees' overspread, withdraw by season but don't needle the already flanged bones of winter.

ii

Goes as sheltered as its non-preserve can inhere, a time to crouch horizon's diving root at foot, bundle that hurdles leaves mapping about the edge. Pinned shirtlets from the same disfold, fluctuating asymmetry in tremors across even-waged leaf. A ripple bodes enhanced border as preparation for under-breach (root) not now an outreach: yards to the crossing spell of so much bivalent breadth. Standings of waves risen wrap themselves round any subjacent lamination: let offset particle bite and suck the granule of its adherence. A lattice warrant of ipse scours idem off its blocked scaffold as the inherent lath-lace the former of it is: until all such trees can be what they lie on (once tall with holding up what they lie under). An intra-foliar froth of shelter flaking onto rungs of the wood. Layered turbulence, not piled florescence, of the field's clipping leaftext (thin client) to prolapsal edge: that leaf-end is scaled a higher pause, a larger offer. Just as screens of origin aren't skins of shade. Laminae shift because their primaries don't vertically sift but accompany a lifting out of entrance onto the unopening. Does this curdling of leaf-edge add towards root-patience, though cradling as this is persists hedge in the field array only? The leaves lay long open for the scraper buds of the trees' simmering origin, a leaving ligature, *to* field. A ramification broad blade which allows rim divergence to sift in secret. Infra-exudation which isn't the initial insulator by turns super-foliar, but how leaflets do the film of origin only unscarfing at horizon what holds them hold out to it. The beginning is palisade and spongy tissue, a whole roller-face "leaf, print on life" drooping provisionally on support fieldlessness below. Between air of heaven, and earth in furniture, is layer of leaf, which distends *along* its fingers suspending hold: what holds it there (earth) not what it gave way to (heaven) and not what it means (field). As horizontals will field horizons to come by foliate, which not being *woven* veil is means of updraw for vertical concision. By which a field *stretches* better than it extends.

iii

If the limbs of the tree were to inscribe directly on the field of leaves it would go barren in mesh, not a sourced veil given over at a yet poorer space of yield. The limbs not themselves dipping to earth share the hatches of leaf-field, are boughs *under* edge: its offering them a rimless refrain, how drooping from field at veil faltering precipitates branch and stalk. A pellicle of the onrisen which staffs the supportable, how field promised horizon is not stalkless to: is primal for the nearest derivative, stack-up whose beneath is deferred-to from the outstretch above, allowed a whole pillar of trussed supplement. That origin is a loose shawl over the skelloid: that skelloid lately supports what was *its* support from a field always over itself. The far spectacle is the facing side of protection, as not naked bears on opening at the closely secreted mouth, a placation fetching draped arch before it will pleat in the stiff runnels of tree upcrust. From which, postfield to posts, of tree canopy by which. Not a single switch over, a field in leaf is sufficient to the offer of primary support going beneath an initial covering, both in full draw of horizon, by which an edge is textured to end at a vertical tip, way across the saggy field but resting below its apex. Covering not so much a zero of the supportable, elates encroachment only where its field narrows to root at the ford-horizon. Concession of leafage is its folding of horizon over each previous shoot it hangs from. Dust of leaves in risings not yet layered to stalk:

the wavings pro-horizon must first rust field onto particles blind enough for vertical alley. Unsingular in particle were singles by leaves on the vertical boss of yet to be tree. Farness (up) to the curtain of origin we only seam nearer, suspension instanced in a hung-over, rooted out of a field's nearest counter-imparture. Attentive curtailing over branches bracketted back to that first in leaf deal-out by which they were given to be stronger than origin, which had still to separate the seal-out from leaves of its providing the field of its dividing. A curtaining among the insistence of leaves in which a secondary can give to be primordial in support mode, so leastly in process touched to a local grove of trees. It is field opening not shadow but translucency of grain *onto* opening, far as tall ground got to foliate it in its own time of debitance.

Envoi: late leaves

Willow: *darting bills*

Alder: *spade corrugate, shield surrogate*

Sycamore: *flat flagons off*

Beech: *tiles of sheilings*

Lime: *wipes read on the palm*

Poplar: *sprays of dries*

Ash: *fingers in grapes*

Oak: *early crick, curl as shoal*

Envoi: early leaves

Willow: *buckled propelling intact*

Birch: *wetdust to pebbles*

Sycamore: *if mingled unshingled*

OPEN WOODS

2005

La verticale . . . le prolongement
A travers toi
De la sphere terrestre

Eugène Guillevic

Trees, curled
follicles

Of all the earth

Simon Perril

Es dificil llenar un breve libro
con pensamientos de arboles

Eugenio Montejo

1: URBAN WOODS

Competitive dereliction sets full sticks, pining the abide in assault. Not a mask of it packs green that isn't frontal score absolving a décor foliar nearest, almost the compassion it can't open *from* us: basis for overtaking deals opening trees aren't arrayed in.

re the nourishing, is it
an urgent stock alert?
lost to hosts
packets the term
a visit each

Calm block this low, trees sow down onus with a species rating screened row upon row. Urban lofts do this for tree-mass, the town's hum exhumed home whose expansion goes seriously unending when in plant. Shaded with buried. The tended branch at its slowest from roomside over, give view its bough-stream and ply out along one-way valve. The city lies in warning of its unsorrowing cladding, bark shingle seeks horizontal tray at the slots of dispensation.

moody how guidescape
is leafstock captivated rapt
within the category your
starter glades beat
their fronds woodily

Urban conversion areas throw sacred grove, have seats impliant with the Open, stacked for place across pulse of local salve. Stowed in the ahead until there are settlement scenes we can offer trees their crowns, openly centred around their streeting. Tree bulge yearns component as soon as touched for bud. Regressive north-spire type, slumped arc of the commercial/boreal. More scarcities next teeming, more aground to scarcity next rootlessly nearby: blunt post mode of a tree opening. Old trees ensue surround in suburb-repose dynamic, go the way they got of isolate munificence, no longer stipulating the seed core of a woodland openness.

stemmed by lawn in leaf
staves must branch
slight to amenity
with voluminous nest-segment

Respiring initial additions, treed to a wild junction the filter's violence padded in suburban hard splay. Sanctionless that the remitting agency is prevailing seedless. Who fares whose props are funded to a belt? Where woodland disappeared, disappointed as never opened, fringes siphon off what fields the trees openly were until shaded for a reserve built outward just so far. No one is saying it wrong in human concentrates, but how ubiquitous should be the teem? Plant capital attached to opening ground not by any access grown to account. How far should trees of it string habitats out of themselves by which they aren't plantable?

lichening the back of us
grew to warding forward
infective niche, pitched
like a needle of undertakens
remnant with acceleration

Fading not to but off very green dark, a long leisure of accustomed shade, slipping to highest forest on behalf of. A wooded stream of rungs to quantify at home for the best resting branch over, no draft of the simulations but will exact secondary ripple first bring leaf-flow. To put a roof on a tree disassembles the house, to put trees over an uncovered home dissembles how unweathering the sky has become. How deep park references a landscape's entirety. The human tree loathes by its bounds, loans out an open impress of the woods, typology of a sill it is all window to.

filigree patent, then neuro-
arborial, a leaf bulk
fed urban flanges, tangents
enfilade the casuals
of woodland striving

What is from shelter-belt immediately extractive? A whole tree needed to consign an access road. With sealant bypass driven through ancient woodland, the opportunity to repose on yourself is how natural processes expire, to be ridden into all that passing. By roads that meanly dip to hedge however the headlights stoop through massive middles where woodbrush is magical in its cage-rates of alarm. Road paving throws up tree regime. The feed-packs are occasional puncture with nil runoff, traffic impermeable once under leaf cover.

city grazing less a tree's
enemy than its appealed
irritant, browses an open-
ing gaze astride

As route is related to rupta a common breach round woods supports factor. Woods comprising such lesser wastes need not be felled if their preservation is throughly speedful. Pickets at the stake of, until rafters know hugely this no-longer-ripe-for-cutting, readily steals out with suburban sleeve. Gloved and likely trunks of obstruction. Richer in regional performance given the stack of greenspace: high because these nurture packets are storage, or not by wilting trees soaring the stage of. Keys of shelter per node, weakly dense multiway trees.

nominated shadehouse that sev-
erance blinks a manège so
starkly parked in zone,
paraglade by protocol, the
urban to woodland salient
speculatively pre-netted
protractive of its pre-
dicament's gauze

Are the woods weak enough to recordon us now for the space we primordially breathed them outside? To enleaf a post-cutter culture until these shades clarify the bitter plain without being bright by clearing? They are openly failed agencies steering into us. Urban in semi-habitual, caller recognition in sworn sequences of glade: how towering extrapolations of sky can't be taller than our volume of assent, but it is all a ribboned arching, trees to get by frequent relief.

can invoke enough re-
seeding/unbedding
us the wood crisis? short-leaved
fault shipped to selective
urban sleeping beside
tasks of green outline

Creating fenestral woodland is caved with success, the habitat means are swung into embrasure. Failings taking well for onset, maturing deadwood drains this stirless so openly at its curve of hold plus stiff meta-find. Visit forest expectation sites as if a composite *un*felling could advance on a wide front, billets tipped for a park. Fashion is fleeting output of large native woodland, its butt opening and then severed facially.

personally plant trees by rack
forget to cut them down to standing,

woodland steeps hidden in vault
descry domestic at human default

Re-establishment at woodside daily marshalled by close folds of degradation: to fork the isolation thimble upto the suburb sitting on branch-end. No significant plants will spike urban fringe unless embedding a planning gain, crave of value-cyst innovates belonging to stain. Waste accorded woodland fee over again, be it well-stocked in the commission cycles: allowing city tents to be the drapes' over-sky for whatever living ruins heal and can't be allowed so much abstraction this year. We are people-radiant in the location use we take from forest and spoke out amid the gapped blockades of wood choice.

nature typed out of ripeness
writes a zone in:
multi-use woodland sieves
referent cores of surround

abrupts of restoration, the
tall dipping-stations, deferent
role steals into gift
thriving chains of region
no longer self-stocked

Patchy location by retribution from the disdaining habitats which remain generous on front-lit call, depends off suburb matting on habitual amplitude, newly assertive that the edge dreams out a braiding sheltered weakly tall. What inflictive distance between our parasitism and our home? Should trees be called to span it, infill their own vistas until vocational, or be companions of the deep shelter monopoly seedcrime?

so few forest remnants
on suburban pennant
species-area wove a
plus population screened
from group by group:
beg tree the overheads

neighbourwoods advise cap-
sulation, this access adore
us down unmeshing pores

Open woods and nearings, their stance of cloying reductively unclear, that we have about us. Young second-growth forests are currently lacking the suites. Closet space begets high canopies without a single desire intact: nesting by glazing free until they dazzle off the rate of opening. Province is niche of the models, devoids are recreations correctly divagated, until diversion symmetrically changes everything. Asymmetry expected the stirring but not to within here the swirl of reciprocity: without the open reversion which would have guided to this entrance.

urban flange woodland
a hard plate but a
cutting instep of following forest

alder splash over rushed soil
in edge of city brush:
as though fall-back
given its possible
were let open woods throughout

woodland of urban or peri-
urban screens, that invention
with empty coming invites
the plots of overhang:
bridges by shortage of projection

2: ANCIENT WOODS

Halving the correlation with ancient descent lives in a simple city of coppice slicing the fluctuation between adventive workings and the primordial. Over here juvenile sentries start shavens long ago tracing up their stools until the assarting put still greater store on a bare use of broken stone, arable soils taking *their* slice out would pincer any young ancient cycle. Over there woodland canopy reverts to grow above handling with incaution of coppice to high forest deserving immemorial frame.

silva modica, silva minuta
youngest in standards waver
giant bites over ridings
stubbings from split hagg

As forest became copious wood culture the trees were hushed behind territories of the periphery. Ancient forest hadn't been impenetrable but proportionally the known visits were raked into clearings: all the rest a protective cone travellers had hard staffing to cross.

sparse penetrable, lesser
branches attacked as relief
from undergrowth, trees
smell small, low branch
in the nose of riders

As field narrative open woodland had the fuller pastoral fantasia over what splays out ground rising by rising than the severer open bays of geological horizon. What fits species into ancient woodland is we are certainly restricted to it, folded within the certains of a strict future above our exposed (ex-poled) skies, clean passage through an iridescent marsh of descent. Trunks casing with us branchless until defendable over half their height. Understorey of hornbeam with a hollow mosaic of younger trees still gangling in the gaps: the hows of a history of the woods, have shown them to the hours.

ancient tree spites relit
dissection in original key
correct origin cut to board
wood fescue on skeletal brown
soils, spores tokenly at pasture

Irregular starts of medieval wood in shapes of let or need, a scanning nape or steep retreat. Population fluctuation indicates along earliest edges too stressed a time of zoning to look back much further how soon they came and were deprived in the recoverables. Forestry will replace woodmanship, a single spire off multi-stemmed stools or shingle clasping the pasture. Sinuous or zig-zag, to their own jeopardy well-stripped peninsulas of mainland trees extended across the withdrawing bays, expend their smooth lines over rocky coast. These work at plenary figures of never leaving the woods they move through. Populace follows widespread spares of woodland until whole trees put sparseness out to pasture. From 16% at the time (1086) to 6% today: can losses like these learn what becomes of any figures for wood *exposure*, how it opens to our forebears without simple erasure? Woods were the only extensional duct alternating agriculture by not depleting how it might be embraced, native weak environing despite retreatant speculations. These wouldn't have been the counter-predominances which *could* settle on an inheritance of our current access-ratio.

maple crabbing up through haw
birch dispel willow
rowan limes between ditches
tilling a wilding's service

white coal in well of
dark bark, that lordings
long escaped this coppice-
cycle, tenantly they out-
subsist sharp agistment
bollings are ridings are times

Semi-ancient naturals mimic the resemblance of common replacement. Erosion of tender or sloped ground where pastoral overload detours the forest. Originary subterfuge only exacted in the nows of assuagement turns resistant to anything but hungry priming. To cope an earth already dealt out, relearn its stealth in the openings no longer adjoining us, send leap-frogging back the anticipation that only retrieved start owes growing to a head what latterly industrial plantations are sowing linear from. A petitionary member of the wood layer remains in old-field network, long periods of existence set to a particular past in its yards. Dominance varies, fails or consolidates in pockets.

tablets of association, how
the ancient siphons forward
its retro-faltering at
swathes of the future:
proximity core sallies
acceleratory its sanicles
into late quarters

Old woodland with its continuity of loss has led to what little of the useless *un*broken grows up beside the more productive shatter, a sparse intact infinitization. Micros so akin in dust of germ give germ they de-figment, scatter their seams of remission over disjunct successions, the trans-massive evanishment. Deliberate damage of existence wears down to expository stands: that trees have fallen openly is how unsevered root-plates know upturn, obtain primordial angle.

soever private how forest-
land came of age in, parcel-
ization because industrial woods
process ancient castes
of more grafted barrier

Forest cycle will emplace on any given past, asynchronous swatch able to last out the pitch of cover to cover, shift the sheer of ground onto vertical mosaic in which a relatively calm disturbance regime can envelop over a long edge, its fine-grained parent encroaching. Steady states within the principal smallness area. So it is woods source their game, dispense wild fruits, hesitantly unremoved a pleasance which lintels the view. Enclave of small branchings of time, the modern plantation is a poor analogue for pre-settlement forest except by descent through coppice scarcity.

no neglect of the reviving
remanent stress, claimant
is possible remanié, *ie* not
closing a replica:
same high field collars
the ancient craning
of released woods

Recent woods are species-poorer than old shaws, assisting the ignorance of how we are to follow the same polity of variety for our borrowings, living the game on. Can there be a time-poverty of opening rarer still in its special inclusions, that scarcity will keep cover to the commonest horizon whose approach seeds subsequent faltering through ages of recognition—such is mono-shelter? Pausing under the mantle until the outside leaf opens, outer side from sore retro-porch of its own.

low historical intensity and
not the minimal past, press
towards opening in sequence
of harbourable use, any stop
or calendared rod out in
planted grain of time-temperance

How late in sway can woodland ever become once it has hollowed up a rigid standard in lacking so much, what with combing the stacks it slits neatly into living vertical veins, the canopy overtow? This slackness which a pre-urban armature protects in the shunt to distribute plenitude new trimly sought? It can be as premature as an active scarcity of opening too fully for the expanses of substitution to be sited ecotonally, *ie* to overtake tree pasture is to be stalled within the plant tunnels which have so readily let the opening abstain behind.

forest ratchet on a chain
of chrono-pendants that over-
hang bite so tree-upright-
ly, times claw *by* tenure
according to remoter unstolens
which only lately give
slips to the covered
way: pristine records be-
taken with obsolete absences

mostly de-restricted, re-
quitals freely slow
how closer of loosened
butt sows cleared relict stand

3: OPENING WOODS

Where woodland is generator the stimulus might be a seared interior, there flames of clearance don't invoke passage. This mode of opening shakes out the rides, goes over exposure through adherence to sheer vehicle of site. The clearance frame would otherwise miss a wide sampling interval: how no path in wasn't this way prohibitive, instead its unsealed singulars (signless in tree order) were openly forwarding the preventive. A resistance opened by its screens, near enough to parse how this poor-in-channel is topped, tapered to convergent openness. The empty cubicle of a leaf-rim gets packed into opening by resting the means of. Lintel quanta of green-scarred admittance.

how grassing into open woods
like these has them commoned,
summoned, the spearing of trees
kept sharp by fire

are not *all* true relicts
because filtered by their
failure to disperse:
the good colonist is
due to its height
of oftener burnt shadow

The composing process of secondary woodland *does* overstay when it rewrites the profile of pre-clearance vegetation. Being uneasily ajar is revision slighting a climax of arena: arena otherwise not patient with any cut-through not itself but a porch-approximation of horizons. Horizon look towards you once you have seen loose-screen continuation in envelope. A probable diversity in fate of origin but intimate unit in the clearing swerve by which openness errs and transfers. As though nature produces coppices without shields of exclusion, but with unpierced films of admittance. Isolation by dwelling-series in build-up: the edges can no longer be accidentally looked for, coverts must be ungropingly stooped from. Presaging a way through other than taken can be to *un*expose openings, long course of a brink at which, once opening by trace was too impaled on horizon ever to trample out its retribution.

orphaned onto slits
leaks a healing counter-
spill out of ways-in

woodthroat dispersal
to aspergent flicker
of gridless leaf

holly trees tell winter food
stunted by the wild
sheltered at a shunned gate
in cleft of steading =
a history of openness

To be among woods in seasons not brooking what is standing from rootless (unopenable) stones. Tree cover might develop another tractability than density. Charcoal platforms have their extraction days, the sawpits a ubiquitous breach in the bank. Fragments are leavings but remaining in if ever hit, how open the trees are, bidden strike with ghosts like any token departure chain-wood. To be shredded is to be self-pollard, subsequently flushed with a new looseness of growth. We don't yet tolerate big dead branches above us but can exonerate the open box of the crown, spars posted beyond closure. Special in place divides less through incision than by creasing its filter-lanes in the unspecial. No mean actor of the clearing, with no need to go stealthily between woods, steals out to an openness slighter than their rival expansions. To find that fallen coat still over us, where openness is push green key, will unlock its lapse to you once no partition slides off the crown.

to be rich in trees may be
to be poor in forest affront:
colonisers (pine, birch, larch)
take stride from light:
continuators (beech, fir)
need shade to be at the outset

dead beech leaves won't
suppress young spruce,
acacia savours oak succeeding
inhibits pine from weeding

Forest doesn't arrive a barrier but at zone-attractor of the least, specified lessening is soil so resultant of overspoil. To appraise forest not by arrayed surface but by numbers of intruders it can find the feed of, how woods gratefully intercede not to be determined by exposure. Not materials as the spaces to be covered by trees, but a zone of reserve whose access falls dim by ulterior opening. A hollow which allows the weightlessness of prime obstruction to settle here. Where any opens are chastened by claddings so far into intervals as interval isn't found alone but within feathery clothing, accessory duct of spread to welcome. From clearings to a harvest of the coverable. Participate opening without emptying a tree's primal follicle pimpling earth before it revolves. Timber on a long, non-local cycle, the frond of distribution. Primordial matter (the khora) timbered as stuff, relict habitat, the immanent semi-shade off gloss.

done-rooting sieves out-rooting
a way in gone among in-
sufficiently fed with surpluses
coppice after the fourth bud
from timber how forest runs

Felled trees amongst the woven chink: unfelled trees can be pleated for opening but the entry *through* fold can't be matted into the weave itself. Horizons will bear so long as there remain woods adjacent to the charges of sky (ahead intrudes immediacy that will bulge towards strikable head). That woods don't concede access once open to what needn't admit the passing room to live through. Most of the trees lying out are ahead of it. But heeding porous solids of the open which slake this channel of reserve, invisible, humbly diagressive, they themselves do pass. Extrapolation is woodland fragment, as surmise peaks for its less natural: authentically the break of, but opens one crossing side to the other.

turn the load over between
havening and like-quieted
woods, deduct these opens
from forest induce bestrewal

a hurtle cascade of blistered
stases, deaf bruising
in the hushwoods
woodland pulse and setland peace

To vindicate drawing out limits until they glint horizon-mark, trees have had to be scored from where opening lays on them its tightest wedge. Free circulation comes to aerate its flouting of any opening that is by range alone, until all that scarification is made diffident going *into*, *ie* entrance may be regressive in having been overt just one side down the external. Forests forced to shut to the wood trade betray required closure to an open closeness not harbouring ingress as solely *this* style in. Permeability is passage but openings commonly dilate by remitting the direction of admission. How do you "leave open" the woods so that their horizon also invites outgrowth to stay overhead, simply as coasting the site of donation? Included at a primordial seclusion, cast broad into a lesser outscattering, or rupture onto the *opening* of a gathering.

light selection of our thinnesses
as significant shade under
closed, shared conditions
charged edge buffers ratio:
redundance, but confluence, of keys

Disruptive profile overtakes unless some opening out of itself breathe lesser make-ways. Woods always the hereditary enemy of receding grassland were also the wide pursuing spine of *its* incorrigible defile of opening. Ancestral terror of obstruction here releases margin along contour, the very seam of exposure marked by a brush-obstinacy: tree company written in deep on funnels of thinnest earth pursues openness further now than across a leading out over empty fertile plain.

solicitude of the woods
pieces in taller scantling
trees poorly started
might hinder envelopment
so poorly parted gives
a sphincter to openness

It can't be denied the treeless agglomerations how they for a slashed part shut forth the textured opens of the woods. Memory of trees hollowing close, fallow wrap round a stance to be open, already filling right through the parted standing. Slow to saturate with torrent glare, fork-whipped in lieu of gate but leaning unspilt. Dedication for the weak incising margins ambivalent once they unfurl: woods conceal their hidden edge until blunt glade opens out of unglassy encounter. How a shallow hollow will close in small fenced pilots on the slopes: oak/ bracken by bramble hooks vertical to copse.

embowlment of site
staves tending access
billets on the surpassed
side of containment

within the coppice
no pan value
of equal surface

a lowly amount of profusion
how forests yield:
unbroken in the grain
unsealed in the texture

Openness as percentage between, not a desert of naked sky but its brush gap insertions which woods strikingly put *below* canopy level: laterals not polar to verticals but winding between masts among the unreleasable poles of shelter. Forest reversion that woods open a discontinuous dressing of earth which a light of shelter shaves through to. Isolates, margins of field, so that dressed light can stalk a terrain beaten into flecks of uprights. Minimal with exact link already outside what a shelter recollected might derive from, were it not for the horizon-blink of open cover. Open source, this greeting convoy to abeyance. Sparsely distributed to be immediately recognised doing something to horizonless opens, threading them on strong draw, or edgelessness which now, free of obstacle, waits steeply without crossing.

unvacant woods where trans-
mission isn't one stay over
but many days torsionally open

commoner owed ford than pro-
tection crosses to shelter
how soon the thrown-opens
are not raided

Infrequent origins should be planted outright because their distribution rarely passes to more distance than far awning. Clouded soils until punctilious woodland stands by the frequency of what is over it, why a roofing air is sharply clustering: only mono-thresholds remain harsh penetrants. Let it corridor in from leached-out ground towards fantails of the covering, shelter is wide sail before radiant ex-radicals. Include the semi-stable fibrillation, embed the out-ties shaking into tree.

conducing granules of the open
award a semi-natural infill

stands translocate forest
incentives, plant existing
stock to distant sources

dendrolattice or dis-
tributed nest still
attributed to this
vestal grain

How softwood canopy is being infiltrated by broadleaf condensing opens. Spruce afforestation a wall to outcall. Lets in the differential blockage which is openness seaming the partings that run texture to cover. Where heartwood loads up de-tract onto forest pact at each openly arising: transects of site maintain a shelter interchange. Thin nutrients poor as soil is open give blinds to highest variety of piercing, ward *into* whatever hunger is overt approach. Then foliar species may rest the gap between composite and cluster. Large expanses of ground tend to shift their own major obstacles: minor votaries the way out through staying under trees.

extra woodland response by
"glowing" passage at a pittance
of the inward receptiveness

low stem densities with good
visibility into close crop:

opens the shadow
of overhead verge

green branch to place
on the vanished crest
best of a *layered* height
still open unapprised

Trees provide for lesser scales of the open just what they wave in with lanceolate attractors, a motion of admittance long after it was shadowless universal arena. Whether to be created over large areas by a single event with foliage: a full house of gaps between surpassed singles of instruction. Where unnaked ground is by that much more open to sky going calling over edge, the hollow wrap of foliage is unapparent until horizon telescopes.

usual face pattern spurned above
openly weaving boughs
intended onto hollows of crown
as traits run to convexities

Woodland to be planted in the next 50 years is set to accrue mourning, not simply because highly containment-dependent but on everything which presses the open to come out of. To bring a different ravage to bear on a damaged landscape, smearing the fluted frictions deep between lancet plantations. Isolation *does* effect seducing, not every corridor will automate the greenways: the amenity line never wholly disanimate but rigid for choice until simple not to select *for* openness, the compaction being already extremely overt. Interlacings reinforced with bramble and thorn bushes, curbing any straggle to be through, but remaining at different *spates* of the protection woods. Native woodland rounded up in a *scatter* of small woods, habitat mosaics have set up their edge: buffering is what the environment suffers through surviving an unexposed and undegraded openness.

woodland ensign rarely stark
what sharp opens do
in its feathery blank

regular disturbance genu-
flects complexity, rich lop
promulgates uneven prop
exposure tucks under
by not fearing into

Human intervenience dries out the vessel of protection, drainage is by dispersion of road stopped up by trees so openly crossing. Those bare-pole brownearth sites bedding over shale, rankers by their silent rooms of tallness over grit, open source of rapidest induction of low-energy future which has the stratification to crawl (if covered) over inventive para-stasis. Blockage at this grid not to be understood across the plains as open slot: green-light guidance with bare ground is given *from* the canopy. Retention of thinnings left handy for failed planting, the open about its business, inexposable uncertains. Averaging across tall storms the fine root turnover.

small-tree material, a readi-
ness of consummation, steady
pores open the pole stage
mast crop sites with no
kernel of removal

Tree planting put captive on site to answer a history of opening-with, increases diversity by protection outlet. Cries out to distinction the releases beneath tracery, distributing each gap as couloir rather than mapped rent: an open not to look out from but gaze within blinds of furthers, arching at the incursion of the other, how slightness shelters what is not its own overfield. Contiguous gap being the lining of gap, blade through blank in the co-separations of among.

openness at wedge jams
good gap to leak scarce ad-
mission of door on floor

Stripping down ensnared flight, which a ladder of compression launches, more as bole casting off dome: lift earth openly *upon* by piercing through pole. Lose the emptied of being-open to what falls through loss by remaining upright, pine-high in the eye of needle, openly rich interval never closed by that mite of interruption which a tree has spread on ground. One membrane open arc onward can be timed in the matrix of rims and cloaks of earth. Pressed not sealed by the plant of vertical welcome. As trees no longer guaranteed a world we stood outest to. Today a tree shelters leanly because open as we are, not learning the forest's ravage until its holes are a cry of scarcity. A turbulence of being hushed to limits, opens what a peripheral non-turbulence repeals.

> fold of isolations onto
> separative invergence shade-
> endows, as *some* of the way through
> grain of leaf over ground

These opens coming in like ecological insertia. Pioneer openness has already thinned *itself*, lodges between heartwood with a vacancy not to be in deep. Which isn't desertification by consistory, simply quite helpless making entrance, insistent when all spindly fixations lie against the sill. The highly open can never be *lightly* wooded. A wilderness of anchorables, another way in forgets holding on which this covering admits to horizon, opens the hook recalled during our primal insulation and lightly shrouded out.

> woods try for first player
> abandoned lanes gather like

openings on slopes or bluffs
stuck with yawning strategy
in such low scoring

This semiwild transitive penetration, terraces cover the way by relinquishment of all the least exposed you have violated through wholes of sides: that opening narrates a no longer vanished compression. Trunkless apart from tunnelling the green legs, brushy fielding in at the tiniest inevitability of forest, not a stunted visor lifting but along its avoidance-into. Scarcity of cover *does* draw the open toward.

go quotiently that woods promote the failing
acres, open woods are near you
sheer of your full cycle

MOVING WOODS

2005

For (and partly from) Stanley Wood
and Pen Hill, Gloucestershire

It cannot be merely a question of an unmysterious interval . . . between these trees nearby and those further away

Maurice Merleau-Ponty

to meet with moving woods,
And walking Forrests

Macbeth (William D'Avenant), V.iv

If the forests weren't to have been cleared for a continent, these scalar posts wouldn't have been a force to displace in rising. Only covered terrain shows lightly mobile, over the whole envelopmental distance.

habitat target
moving past the hurts
fast in tree stases
the only stopping
that trees began to move

Very small patches lead to concentrically scattered instability in the woods, openly interfere with such shards migration quickens until persistence of movement is drawn *over* clustering.

transfocal setworks
clothed in signs of in-
coming periphery, less
desymbolized than strips
of rolling the forest

Woodland increases its percentage in the fewness of its felt locations, contiguous loss if active advance preys on green stealth. Tapes of fragmentation open the moves without unravelling the going.

Highly mobile limbering the ascent to a counter-migration? Timber-splice crosses the grain of exile, no protective intersections mitigate *unless* they move as the shelter roams.

the trees well up from
their stillness position
the motion ridge
of offering site

Limit-behaviour gets in densely but not under the clip of insertion, is a new race to the movement of close foliage. Masts across a waste not outwardly off any reel but like unspent linkage recycling the approach itself, means a cylinder is to partials. Trunks move off the roll, not on the turn.

hanging brush
rotates at outward tip
always vertical, this way
interrupts *at* the turn

I must find the figures of what has actively been left to reducible forest stripped para-intimate, gentle-exiled a world tall over, semi-naked from origin half earth in the stalking folds.

a disposition like
embraceable motion
in whose tree-core
fore-structure
throws it shelter

They slope, cool dust until slippage, to the hanger but move as we are, motes of shade. The openness of hanging woods is motile descent, as slopes rotate an unvarying ration down the vertical.

Alongside, once through trees, the motion looked too dressed with infinition, but what slides is to show what covers is moved, the jump to a layerable until horizon's.

pull tree across tree
without easing the lull
of shelter, distribute
rapid woodland
racing the encroachment

A tree-mania in lieu of hope in the woods, but
too lightly striking a step of root over root
for any 'fixist' excess to get blindness from its
attrition to place: where the no-hold (dazzling)
gives an *un*stripped step.

rare random habitats
moving about common hold
accelerate imperceptible
remnants unwrapping
steerable surround

Accompanied origin which crops edge for horizon: the boundary stripped at unporous juncture sharing out the overarching travel of it. If tree moving tree does a preservation run, tree holding tree is an unrevoked pursuant.

how woods move through spoils
potent with contaminant agility

static betide fluxes but
hang across in semi-arid
systems, jumper to pinion

Private turbulence of stowing the next move, allowing it incisive travel along the coil of mid-slope. Zonate leaf-jump, crawl goes under a spansion of the woods, short instances ahead of universal distances.

spinal hook
flinging out
motionlessness
aligns a tailing
slow enough to
draw down horizon-pull

Movement *was* disturbed and sufficiently segment-defective, but enough severally if tree-crown relocates where shelter leads its journey scarce to complete beyond primal welter.

offshore sediment
onshore horizon

for simplest collar
prehensile root
polling its hold

Barriers of brush give the moving by remonstrating the threat, speed indicates to empty fuel, accelerates a wheeling plain because not crossing it before one branch interspokes the thin axle play of another.

differentiated intrapath
forages likes of cover
within striding range of
fidelity to non-
transient departure

Substantial in remaining a portion spill-assisted, tread-channels of boundary creasing by root, not to take the step it is of shoot. Leap the runnels and there is pool of leafiest silt, horizon fetches very mobile content off woodland.

motor root will pool
cranes of stems
spread uppermast

it gears what tree
will spine, vertical be-
setting is onto-
logical speed
the stint horizon sprints

Forest accumulators resort mobile to wood pieces culminating key paces. Wood percussive, a thrown simple moves a grown ample, sheltering beckons to be in flight among the strips of participation.

how do trees
slow us to folder
speed, the vertical
stitch in movement?

You knew access to phantasmic shelter, the turn-over of truth along a meta-recess where berooted trunk rolls positive clearance. Movement of plant material from sources of origin, choice of deep cover, *when* to move as strong as the course *in* origin.

Motoric ante-pathways greendate urbanisation? Not desertful projectives off temple threshold, sacral consummates which step the not, but greendead pathos of a travelling burden of reserve.

Letting in vertical manoeuvre during blunt storm events. A motion of heavy forest counts for environmental bearing in the tall run. Spasm of wind in the reversed narrows with broad tree sucking forest canopy. Saplings tumble their side-stems upright, supplied for the corrective outcramming of whole stands.

trees cross moving
companies, thriving west
through piny rows in
north drift. Woods cross
moving search, aim
taller for ground error

humus-mediated moves
trans-latent local
material, a dart lodged
in pitted membrane
fletches hollow and
flies coniferous woods

Curved obstacles with infinite wakes, steadied to vertical thorough plane never cured of flow. The range of sanctuary to sanctuary not just aslope but moving *earlier* than slippage.

Assuming woods display their slow speed entirely in front of: recommended you display moving woods at their calling.

Moving brush to sound you in the open subject base but can't extract object canopies from the low commotion that runs until desert hears: rare is the value of a tree due scarcely to the thirst of moving it.

a blighted clemency of
resonance not induced

slighted, shaded
as it rolls

When woods move, a wilderness is pushing at confines of piloting reserves which are not universals: that the confines travel, not that boundlessness is locked in static opens.

woods for the best
moving shoulder of
vertical resolvers:
were waves forward-
ing ripple mass

degrees of fear posted
through the tipping woods

falls like moving
woodland charged to
they drop between
distance and rest

A body of trees inter-lacks with the world, their hinterspread outlocked into fresh deliveries of each slighting put back into their height.

Woods on the move not because of rebud but in cool limb-sharing. Is there any loud moving off that wouldn't also be a tenebrous scouring?

branches shift way
not as stiff looming

moves but as a wood plunges
before any trees have set out

From covering's bed to the seed of cover in transition of need, woods will move but not exchange, go past their site to the common place of.

The foliage of it deeply subsided if it hasn't ejected its woodland flock: by principle remaining the timber crutch it rooted in motion, what every shepherded extra location bridles.

apartness of the finder-mover
trying to fit a gnarled pace
to a green share
your belonging protocols
as you stole along

Impresses inscriptional launch of moving woods in tidal woodland. Over spilt soils with their seed source intact protruding the sliding inhesion, each tree rudder in sling.

Until woodland shawl is indiscernible, unlike the shift to provider tree. If not moving from cover, covering how far to move: downhill with the up-tends of joints, how it fails any *flatness* of cover.

Trees put to edge what the plains ascend, steeping the cover, sowing the seeds of sinew range, scarped bones stand where they clawed. To relinquish designation accords a wood's own marks of travel, deeply scored into shelter, its seeding linear scarification.

Woods moving back from any spines of advance, deep tactic which cones the niche. Light rises *towards* what bowers trees might travel their shadow in, the glint doesn't sink until an horizon darts.

Moving the woods through no source of light other than an outer split gleam, the husk of dawn carrying inland, lure of shock of post to slice horizon for the flash it throws.

Stopping by trees is many moves at bay of being the flow beside them: complete woods will capture along the ground, staying close to which pitch of screen is in travel.

by moving, woods
you are as stave
to the pro-addition

flail in leaf right along
bitter roof cover
the beam of beating
into breadth
separations of the
bundling germ

Brings unparked hues to the woods, to be in stroke of motion where it is driftless. Trees probe the bendable vertical, roots ride their purchase movable. A chase of the resolution marked on the stretch of placelessness which flares.

Until a tie-move cross the secondary, a space reserved for smaller woods moving out of residence. Primarily beneath tree cover for very spurt, the ocean of localized point.

occlusion clutter
irregular hanging
urging leaf to
run the string

the move took place
a woodrun settles
into slow detections
of its race

Where it goads cluster won't have been just toward its own spaces but a forgiving motion in the field, the foreground harbour which trees are departure into. In a moment, topological precincts arise and model the hang-fast as itself turbulent curtain, how pulse rides full foliage out of hiding.

not to shaft
as slow, to root

the motionful
in true spate

robust segment
distributing statics
out of paying
the motion

veins give lift
to leaf, stiffness
micro-outspread
accelerates a
second prow

Resistance is so projective, the throw against lunge of injectile root. How rooting rides out obstacle inclusion, trees of moving points furrow the grain.

Once given place trees can promote the mass, span a linear face across the moving appointments. Attack the plant as a stake to the ground and the whole earth moves: a blown world perpetually recruited along a glade in local breath.

simple as double-pass
(avoid and evoke)
for distance to be
fast return
(revert and de-yoke)

will fix violations
the tip of any tree
not staying the
violence of a
travelling stillness

How many for open-source appetites? This serious nest, by moving before a series, could grow to like it, invested the whole of a dumped stand in the new. Plant the splint so its zero end will be a stump of flight for your lint of site.

trees ease themselves
on a bed at find
time surrounding it

woods *will* describe
how trees chased back & fro
the hunt to keep margin
on horizon's tail

Not just how trees moved downslope in block, or how they thank their seeds to move their species out of landslip, but how a carved or scarred limb may be journeying lightly the inscriptional salve, second readers of cover.

Landscape has removed scores of trees, mostly by obstruction's due relief, a nomadic vent conservative of stockage. Ask a spent tree to refresh the moving box, and root in cistern will be within ferrying its tissues to fissures.

large trees slewed
the hill by carrying through
with their sleeves' ivy

Moving branch to the sheerest candidature of root, bleached postmodern shadelands, landcare in the slipping sun but rubble sanctuarist: the bias of fit panning before passage.

At a trans-hour, radiance of sun in the universal moves to linear consent any beech-tendrils striating across it: pure white light keeps the ivy in hasp.

Fairness earth/far plain cloaked swiftly near dome under trees, the last filter before an unburied but never exposed horizon.

no counter-stress
but where sliding mass
cleans its country

Brown veils greening out much of the meta-random stabbing towards moving on behalf: strange attractors harmless at the tree neck. It streams a chaos until all waves are for the tortum of being skimmed present.

A stub of green closure tenders the huddle intimately released, hastens glade over spoil, splash of shelter before a soil. Fast succulent layers within dry spools of season, alleviative returns that it moves a day.

Where all that instructed leaf in shade isn't narrow eye but scarce of the fore there is to guide: moves in rueful stride to a going house of roots, the bare motive for it to decide.

bid from breach
scratch through
stretch in healing
theirs for unsealing

a graze of shelter
overhangs the con-
vergence of its
turn to throw

Of each rolling orchard a tree share remits entranceship in the shallow: sequential scatter of inferred way goes between fruiting hollows of the unstoppable given.

Root echoes on the jolt a silent extension to completion, that branch-ends are horizon which *they* move. Towards the stake of it being movement-given before them. Blockades offend trees to the life when they slip through the lateral, not bending more than a lean offer will supplant itself out of vertical slot.

against any ex-foliar
bends and glides
a pole grammar
pressing the statics

a trunk's piercing
how immutable:
placing grows the
motion lineament
featly round it

Now a rod skimped vertical rotation, it gathers at horizontal propensity, without which no field through plantations will lodge the protection's gain play: adjusts to solid-site moves unsawn startups rarely slighting their fast follows.

trees fly to the
slantwood
they can't show
they won't move less

catching root
in that blown slat
where the haul
became faster apart

Sealed on horizon beside a move off soil floors, the bond is showing bolder removal, launching distributory sill strict from a leaf tagging for horizontal height.

Most lost hatchings are world echoes not strayed but filtered by the tree matters moving through it, at each branch delta a mooring swell bounces what the movable knelt.

Hill flanks at convey settlement for unflailing the movement of receive a travelling leaf which brings the whole tree earthable with it.

coil of leaf
quakes best
like simple curl of root

teach for the stuck object
a tree swaying
eased distances
intrusive sender
of interior yards

Its scope moving as whole scape rests on impasse, which to be shelterable overtakes: a flattening of pinnacle until deep relay is a root-run of cut until cramp.

I don't sheet from the tearing, simply pump along shorn tree until primordial acceleration does the covering, sweeping off root any small stayers: poor tall force is moving care enough.

Deck-plenty shooting wide its base beneath arrival, very near horizon was less piped on board than planked immanent by horizontal tree remove: what only then displaces the stages across by its unshiftable vertical roll.

www.ingramcontent.com/pod-product-compliance
Lightning Source LLC
Chambersburg PA
CBHW032055150426
43194CB00006B/539
* 9 7 8 0 9 0 7 5 6 2 9 7 9 *